ALONE

ALONE

Stories & Poems

Robert Cruess

Library of Congress Cataloguing in Publication Data:
A catalog record for this book is available from the
Library of Congress

For
Anne Charter Cruess

*"One always dies too soon—or too late. And yet
one's whole life is complete at that moment with a
line drawn neatly under it, ready for the summing up.
You are—your life."*

— Jean-Paul Sartre

*"Ah, Sweet—The moment eternal—just that and
no more—"*

— Robert Browning

"To infinity and beyond!"

— Buzz Lightyear

Contents

Nor Claim to Eternity

Captain, my capstan   has shattered
Can it matter a whit or less
When viewed from afar
That a soul has no purchase
Nor claim to eternity   that
Place that ideal
Neverending?

And tell me, Captain
What was it like before
The beginning?
Or does *beginning* and *end*
Fail to have meaning?

On the scale of eternity…
We aren't   to be found —
Our souls have no purchase,
Just one burst of time.
Thank you, my Captain
For mine.

Above it All

Ominous clouds   black
Expanding rolling
Roiling Mendota   awakening
Waters from an afternoon nap
Lightning cracks on high   dives
Into Mendota
Its waters a-boil,
Boats struggle with the fetch
Then dash for shore   and
Perceived safety of a distant pier.

So… above it all   up here
Above the fracas and distress
Swaddled in warmth   secure with our coffee
Like gods observing the fate
Of those at sea… we see
the boaters panic   we can but watch—
One boat, then two upended
People who hadn't planned to be in the water…
Now are
Bobbing about with no control…
And then the sky   from east to west
Begins to clear—and boaters' fears
Are upended with hope.

Dreamlife of Angels

well i have dreams too
less grand than those of angels i suppose
but as a human
i can only dream of what i can conceive
and lacking cosmic knowledge and a knowing
of all that is and isn't
i can but dream my little dreams—
dreams that always hold...
    a place of love   for you.

Guernica

Have you seen Guernica?
Nearer to Bilbao than to Donostia-San Sebastian —
very Basque   (and where did they come from?)
and who would bomb
this lonesome Town?   what was the point?
If... you can't even read the city signs... if
they speak pigeon Spanish... who cares?
Picasso —
Picasso cared   he showed the terror
of the German   bombing
    the desperation of the dying... in Guernica.

Guernica... is also...
a massive work   an opus
in black and white that seems bigger than
the gallery   in Museo National Centro
                De Arte Reina Sofia
                Madrid, Spain,
Room 206

Have you sat with the painting?
Have you felt Guernica?

Have you seen Guernica?

Like Souls on a Journey

Pods engorged with seeds   Burst
White wisps   loosed on the winds
The seeds set upon their journey
Like souls searching
For reincarnation —
Above them welkin blue —
Beneath them earthly greens
And ocher browns —
They are free… searching
If only   for a time
Measured in breaths.

Garra Rufa and Maundy Thursday

Let me tell you about Garra Rufa and how it relates to Maundy Thursday. It all begins at Angkor Wat, the World Heritage site in Cambodia. It is truly an amazing place and if I'm fortunate enough, I will visit there again. But back to the story, when you arrive at Angkor Wat, you are warned, a.) Do not let a child, typically a teenage girl, hand you a baby to hold because the girl may run away and leave you with the baby. (The poverty is such that an extra baby is an unsustainable burden. Tragic. The baby looks at you with deep brown eyes, extends its so small hand and… you have no choice… but to walk away), and b.) Don't eat the food offered by the vendors at Angkor Wat.

On the grounds surrounding Angkor Wat, there are hundreds of vendors selling souvenirs, drugs, scarves, etc. and… "mystery food." Our guide had told us that the food was to be avoided, however, I chose to see beyond the advice—I was hungry and the mystery food looked… edible. I ate some(thing), then dodged a couple of young girls pleading with me to just hold their baby for a minute while they rested. I resisted eye contact, kept my hands in my pockets, and got on the bus for the ride back to the bustling tourist town of Siem Reap. It's a basic tourist town catering to visitors who have come from every country on Earth seeking the unique experience that is… Angkor Wat.

In Siem Reap, we walked the streets, jostling with the eclectic tourists, it was like the bar scene in Star Wars as we searched for that "special souvenir." And then we saw something that amazed me—people were sitting on high chairs, like shoeshine chairs except that they had no shoes and their feet were dangling in transparent tubs filled with murky water and… Garra Rufa fish. Really! The fish were swimming around and going from toe to toe of the "patients" and eating the skin between their toes. It was one of the strangest happenings I'd ever seen. The people being eaten had smiles on their faces and willingly paid the plus/minus cost of 20,000 riels (about $5.00) for the cleansing experience.

Based on my religious upbringing, I connected the feet cleansing with… Maundy Thursday, or Holy Thursday and the ceremony at the Last Supper where Jesus washed the feet of the Apostles. This tradition is still carried on by some Popes who will, on occasion, wash the feet of one of the faithful on Maundy Thursday. Interesting, and whenever I've seen the ceremony, I would think about how it might be made "more efficient." In Siem Reap, it occurred to me that if Jesus had had access to Garra Rufa, He could have simply filled a couple of tubs with tepid water and then put the Garra Rufa in charge of cleaning the feet of those shoeless Apostles. He could then kick back with a glass of wine and watch the Garra Rufa do what they enjoy doing.

I was sitting on a park bench in Siem Reap, watching the fish devour dried skin, and ruminating on the merits, or non-merits, of Jesus, using the Garra Rufa on Maundy Thursday—and then—I was given a *sign.* I suspect the sign was given, as a guide to my thinking about Jesus and His handling of Maundy Thursday.

The "mystery food" had roiled my digestive system and I was about to lose control of my excretory functions.

No details will be forthcoming because it was a public embarrassment to have... soiled myself in downtown Siem Reap. I got the message.

The point is, Jesus, even if Garra Rufa were available, would have handled the washing of the feet exactly the way He did.

Our days are numbered

how many more
    good years do i have?
if i imagine, say 10,
it seems like a very small number,
but if i choose
to see the years filled with days,
i would have 3,650… WOW!
even i
might achieve
more
than you might believe
if i were given…

a few thousand days.

Selkie

I saw the Selkie
Lumbering down
The weathered seaside path.
 He had been told
 By the voice of the Sea
That his Earth-born sons
 Were set free of life
 By a man who called
 Morag his wife.

It was Morag that bore him
 Three, selkie-sired sons
 And it was Morag's Earthly husband…
 That had them all undone.

"What right," the Selkie bellowed,
 Had any Earthly man
 To claim those lives?"

Then down the path
 The Selkie saw
 The old salt stumble
 Humbled by Scotch

And the Selkie in righteous rage
 Then tore him limb from limb
 And cast his parts upon the Earth
 So as not to besmirch…

The Sea.

Up Out of Texas Rising

The sky opens wide as sky can get
The red earth of Texas flattens in four directions
West of Amarillo and East of Glenrio
Blue of the firmament drops down to greet us

The red earth of Texas flattens in four directions
Tornados gather in the distant light
Blue of the firmament drops down to greet us
We and tornados rush toward collision

Tornados gather in the distant light
Shelter or luck will confirm our fate
We and tornados rush toward collision
We turn North… tornados veer South

Shelter or luck will confirm our fate
West of Amarillo and East of Glen Rio
We turn North… tornados veer South
The sky opens wide as sky can get.

One Mississippi...

Seconds gather and morph
To minutes   minutes to days

But seconds
   are the building blocks
As atoms make molecules,
Seconds build days —
Myriads more… and there is your lifetime.
They are meant to be touched   held
As they pass.

What did you do   what was done
As they passed?
Were there magic moments?
Ones that lingered   imprinting
Their passing   their passion
On your mind?
On your soul?

September

In the chill of autumn breezes
Huddling on the summer porch —
We watch the leaves leaving
Shrouded in colors gathering
In celebration   of a season
Well lived.

All geese and tourist birds ponder
The long flight south   while I
Imagine snowdrifts and icy winds…
The flies and mice consider moving in

And so begins
Our dream of Spring.

The Centurion

Jesus
Saw him coming
He looked down and into
The Centurion's eyes
As a belamed horse
Through its eyes pleaded
With his master
Who loves him   to take his life —
And the Centurion
Took pity
Upon a god on a cross —
He raised   his euthanasianal
Sword and drove it
Home through the heart
That bled
For him   the Centurion.

Walking to School in San Miguel

A dove alit
On the woody bougainvillea
I heard the flutter
   Don't look up
I heard cooing
Of pigeons and doves
Roosters crowing
   Don't look up…
A *wanton brick*
   Upon the path
A *grapefruit rind*
   A gift for the doves
A *bane for* a *man*
   Don't look up
Women on the balcony
   Shuffle their feet
   Geraniums to be arranged
   White and pink
   And pulsing red, but
   Please
   Don't look up
Columnar cedars pleading
   With the morning sky
   A cobblestone went missing —
   Upon the walk
   For God's sake...

Don't look up

Carlo and the Boston Riots of 1967

On June 2, 1967, my friends and I got caught in the middle of the Boston riots.

It all began in 1965 when my ability to pay for my tuition at Northeastern University began to fall short. In spite of saving every penny I could during my co-op job and driving a cab at night, tuition kept rising faster than I could make money. So, when I found an interesting note on the university bulletin board—something to the effect of… *"Looking for a live-in property manager to oversee 15 apartment units in the Roxbury area of Boston—the right applicant will be required to collect unpaid rents and to keep the properties clean—the manager will receive free rent and utilities."* WOW! Free-rent and utilities—that would put me over the hump and with my other income, I should be able to pay the tuition for the remaining two years of college and get my engineering degree.

The property owner turned out to be a professor at Northeastern who had just inherited the apartments from his father. I hate to use the term "slum lord," but his father was a "slum lord." The professor apologized for the condition of the apartments, but as he said, "They are what they are" (very profound) and was I interested, or not?

Having no other options, and with tuition coming due—I took the deal.

Just after moving into my "new" apartment on the first floor, left-side of a six-unit building, my car, *Belle*

Olds, exploded as it topped a hill on the Mass Pike. The block cracked and drained cooling water directly to the engine. It was an impressive death. Belle had almost 400,000 miles on its odometer, about 50,000 of those miles were mine, and since I had paid only $10 for Belle, I could only say, "R.I.P. old girl."

I had AAA come and tow old *Belle* to a junkyard near Worcester, MA. I admit to being sad even more than I was depressed about losing my transportation—no car, no job. I asked the owner of the junkyard if he had any deals on "previously owned" cars, meaning cars that had survived an accident and could pass inspection. The owner seemed sympathetic to my situation; he thought for a minute and walked with me to a 1952, spiffy looking, two-tone, blue Pontiac Chieftain. I was thinking this would be well above my price range, so I asked, "What's the problem?" He said, "After the engine heats up the valves expand and it can be up to 2 hours before it will start again. You also have to use ether to start the engine after it has cooled off. Just pop the hood and spray the ether in the carburetor, run to the driver's seat and she starts right up." "Well," I thought, "I only drive to school or work and I leave the car for several hours before starting it up again and this car is a real beauty and it has only 200,000 miles. So, that begged the question… "How Much is it?" He said, "Fifty dollars," and I said, "I have never paid over $30 for a car." He said, "Did you ever own a beauty like this one?" Now he had me. I was agonizing over the deal when he said, "Look, I know you are in a spot—$38 and it's yours and you drive out of here in 10 minutes." I said, "Deal, let's get the paperwork done."

A few minutes later, I was driving out of the junkyard feeling like a rich man, and the junk guy even threw in a free can of ether. The radio worked, the car was purring—life was good. All I had to do now was to come up with a name for the car. I had an hour's drive to get to my apartment, and I was resolute in my thinking that I would come up with a name for my new car by the time I drove to Boston. I was listening to the public radio station and they were talking about Sophia Loren finally being able to get married to ... Carlo Ponti—"Eureka." I had found a name. The fact that Carlo Ponti was mentioned at this pivotal point in time, was a sign from the gods.

I parked my new acquisition in front of my free apartment on Albion Street, stepped back, and took a good look at "Carlo Ponti." Very nice, I thought to myself, "However, I can't let my new asset look too good, after all this is a poor neighborhood, not to mention that, I was *the man*— collector of back rents, solver of problems, arbiter of disputes, and... the person who took the garbage out on trash day." I decided that I would take Carlo for a ride through some dirt roads at Franklin Park, no need for anyone to think that I was driving around in a luxury car.

Things got better on Albion Street. A former roommate moved in, and in return for his share of the free rent, he helped me with the management chores. It was a win-win situation, and, he brought along a table, a chair, and a TV. Actually, it was just a TV tube without the box, however, it brought in 3 or 4 local channels using just a coat hanger as an antenna. Life was good. We were living for free only a short ride from Northeastern University and we had enough money to cover expenses for our final two years of college. We could see the engineering degrees at the end of the tunnel. We were adapting to life in the ghetto, which these days would be called "the hood." There are, of course, many stories about our two years in the hood, but those stories are for another day.

This story is really about Carlo's big adventure which began on the weekend that we invited women friends from Connecticut to come and experience our... "unique" lifestyle. We also invited a married couple with whom we were friends to also share this weekend that very few, if any, young white people were even able to imagine. Albion Street and the Roxbury hood was a way of life—we got along with just about everybody. The neighbors said hello to us and we to them and we often chit-chatted with the diverse group that shared our lifestyle, although, we knew that our lives would change once we had our engineering degree in hand... we also knew; their lives would not.

On Friday night of the visit, we drove the girls around the hood, let them feel the ambiance, and, as an added bonus, they got to experience the limo-like ride that Carlo provided. For supper, we went to the "Rib Crib." The "Crib" was essentially a shack in the middle of a block in the middle of Roxbury that had been completely demolished in anticipation of... redevelopment. The Crib was filled with smoke—you would walk up to the Crib and yell your order into the smoke, "I'll have six rib plates, four slices of white bread with each plate and extra barbeque sauce on all six." "OK man, gimme $18."

A hand would reach out through the smoke and take the money. A few minutes later, someone would yell out, "six plates, extra bread, extra sauce." We walked over and hands would come out of the smoke and give us the paper plates loaded with charred ribs covered in barbeque sauce that had been cooked over a wood fire. The wood was actually construction debris and we always joked that it was the lead paint that gave the ribs their very special... *sweet taste.*

There were always 50 or so locals and gang members hanging around the Crib and as far as I know, we were the only white people to enjoy this exquisite, Roxbury cuisine. So that was Friday night.

On Saturday night, we loaded Carlo up with the same crew and headed to Brookline for some live rock music and dancing. It was too loud and that made talking difficult and drinking easy. The music was disjointed, and hard to dance to, so that also made the drinking easier. We yelled, told bad jokes, and mostly drank.

Shortly after midnight, I gathered the buzzed group (perhaps drunk might be the correct word) and that included me as the driver.

Once the crew was seated in the car, I opened the hood, sprayed the ether, turned the ignition, and Carlo, with a deep, soothing hum, came alive—it was a beautiful sound to hear. I got out of the car, shut the hood, and then turned Carlo towards home. I decided to take all the back roads so as to lessen the chance of any encounter with the Boston police—I did not want to be stopped after having had too much to drink. I opted to drive over Mission Hill, turn on Blue Hills Ave, then turn on

Dudley and follow Dudley to Albion St.—that was the plan.

I drove over Mission Hill, made a few rights, a few lefts, and came to a stop at the corner with Blue Hills Ave. Holy shit. Everything was on fire—the sky glowed orange, people were running around smashing windows, throwing stones or whatever, yelling, chanting, coming out of stores with whatever they could carry, all the bodies were black silhouettes against an orange world. *What is going on? Is this a riot?*—I stalled the car. Oh, Christ! I have a car full of white people in an almost all-black neighborhood. I can't just stand here—I opened the hood, grabbed the ether can, and sprayed the carburetor. That was a terrible idea. The engine exploded in flames. I yelled for the others to get out of the car. Then from the trunk, I pulled out blankets, rags, and an old sleeping bag all of which I threw on the engine—the fire sputtered... out. Carlo would not be starting for another two hours or so. We stood there hiding in the shadows, nobody had even paid attention to the car on fire. A cab came around the corner and stopped behind Carlo, and before he could back up, I rushed over and asked if he could just give us a push out onto Blue Hills Ave. If he agreed, my plan was to coast all the way to Dudley Street, and with a bit of luck, we would be beyond the riot. The cabbie was a black guy and he quickly saw our predicament, i.e. six stupid, white people, numbingly drunk, standing in the shadows of the worst riot that Boston had ever known, at 2 AM in the morning and their car was... dead. I reached in my pocket, pulled out whatever money I had and said, "Here, take this, I only need to be pushed about one hundred feet on Blue Hills Ave, and then it's all downhill." Cabbie said, "Put that money back man, and

git in, this is your lucky day, I'll do it." "Thanks, man,"
I said, "I owe ya."

We got in the car, I put it in neutral and the cabbie
gave it a push onto the Avenue—yes, yes, just a little
more and there we were at the crown of the hill, I stuck
my hand out the window and waved—the cabbie backed
off and we coasted... right through mayhem, chaos, fire,
smoke, silence, clouds of orange smoke, people running,
silhouettes of people with stuff—and just an eerie
silence like watching a movie, a bad movie—why were
these people doing this? They live here, they used to
shop here, now the stores were afire, looted, it would be
years before things returned to normal, or whatever
normal was destined to be.

The rioters seemed not to notice us as we soundlessly
glided through the mayhem. Were we invisible? Were
they all too busy making fires and looting stores to
notice us? What were we doing here? Why did I ever
think that bringing these women into our world was a
good idea? I **had** to be here... they didn't. I remember
thinking, *"Things will be different—many many lives will
be changed... and not for the better."*

Further down Blue Hills Avenue, there was less
smoke, fewer silhouettes, no more stores to loot, and as
we came to the intersection with Dudley Street, I eased
off on the brake and let Carlo's speed carry us through a
sharp turn on to Dudley where there was an open
parking spot. Carlo came to rest about 50' from the
intersection where I could leave him for the night. We
exited the car. We were only a half-mile walk from the
apartment. Frank said, "Let's get to the apartment and
have a drink."

Return to me

I see you raise
     Your head
As Lazarus
     You are   no longer dead
And how did time
     Unwind
Or be it an illusion
     Within…
     My mind?

May I kiss
     The specter of your lips?

Will you hear me
     When I say,
My love will not be lost
     Might you die
More times than I
I'll always see you touch you…
     In my mind.

You… are always changing

one trillion
is a number   1000 times larger
than a billion   which
is 1000 times bigger than
one million… think about that —

the human body has… 37 trillion cells and
each cell has 100 trillion atoms
therefore each body has +/- 10 to the 27th atoms.
2/3 of those atoms are Hydrogen,
1/4 of the atoms are Oxygen,
1/10 of the atoms are Carbon, and
even with all those atoms   we are…
Mostly nothing... but empty space.
      Trillions of neutrinos pass
      Through our bodies every day without bumping
      Into any of the mass that we are…
or aren't.

collectively our cells
contend with the onslaught of entropy,
disease, radiation, and aging —
each cell must be fed,
waste must be removed   its structure
renewed   and in the renewing,
our memories are transferred to new cells —
not a perfect process —   and
the who of who we are…
is constantly changing.

our heroic cells,
like the Spartans at Thermopylae,
fight on   (though they too shall lose)
to the relentless
march of the universe
toward the endless cold   of endless death.

"All Hallows" Eve

It was Pope Boniface IV
When thinking of becoming
A saint   himself
Proclaimed November 1st
Of every year to come…
As "All Saints' Day"
(Now a saint is a soul
That we know is in Heaven)
And a non-sainted soul,
Among souls whom we know,
Is a soul seeking Heaven, and
They too, by Boniface IV,
Were given their day and date,
"All Souls' Day" on November 2nd.

And all these saints and all these souls
Are loosed on "All Hallows" Eve—
And the world goes guising
To avoid being seen
By spirits unseen.

But I wear no guise,
I'm willing to see and be seen—
Come all you saints, and
Come all you souls… we are one.

From the depth of a healing sleep

she fetal kicks me with her knees
shoves her pillow westerly
toward my head waking   me again
and then   i turn and wonder
am i mad?   or just madly in love?
with the only woman to have shared this bed.
i watch her sleep   now deep in dreams
eyelids twitching   facing
but not seeing   the man
who loves her so.

Awareness

i remember
    playing in endless sand—
    sand by the sea
and confronting waves
    bigger than me—
a boy alone   for hours
    for days
with no more awareness...
    than a fish.

If All Days Were August

We on the porch
Our memories at hand
Look into and through
Our souls to understand

Why all life
Was given this day?

Are these the moments
We were born to live—
If all days were August
Could life ever   have more to give?

La Florida

flowers are everywhere
summer birds twist and spin
   through heavy air
going here
   going there
alighting on flora
with names unknown to me.

my bones revel
in welcome warmth—
sure… they remember the cold,
they've guided me down mountains
on skis   across broad lakes
on skates—
now my bones are happy enough
to walk the sands of a lonely beach
or amble along a flowery,
long-overlooked   path.

Ever Too Perfect

Is the rainbow there
    For the flowers to see?
Why is grass
    Grass?
Or trees   trees?

    All of everything
    Seems to me
Ever too perfect—

Than there is a need
    To be.

Stones

In the fall, after the last leaf
has ripened into earthy lace
and readied itself to nourish
its beginnings,
the ghost trees loom upward
whispering stilled secrets to the sky.

The stones present themselves,
proclaiming their royalty,
their authority
over the fleeting beauty
of past seasons.

They remind us that all life
rises up
in unexpected places.

— Carole Jenisch

The Weight of Time

The Weight of Time
like the decay of leaves
under feet in autumn,
waiting, hoping,
not daring to know itself.

In the silence of the hour
the watery-finned creature
grows its legs
and slides up the rich, brown earth
leaving its warm silky home
to stagger across a barren land.

Stunned, it circles itself
in confusion, unable to call
hope by its name.
Birthing its presence with a breath
it answers eternity's call.

And tired, it rests
In the dry-brown crackling leaves
darkened black
by sweet mystery.

— Carole Jenisch

Blood Money

I wasn't the first college student to have to deal with money issues.

I was always looking for deals on products that I needed or for ways to supplement my income without taking away from desperately needed study time. I participated in "experiments" at many of the local colleges and universities. I would answer questions on any topic that was "grant-worthy" or submit to Rorschach Inkblot Tests.

The tests were easy because there were no "correct" answers. I could say anything that popped into my head and the non-judgmental test person would just nod. After an hour or two of testing, a clerk would walk over and hand me a check. Easy money.

I participated, or tried to, in a drug study where they wanted to give me a drug or a placebo, I wouldn't know which. I would have to take a pill every day and then show up at the lab once a week for eight weeks to have a blood test. Prior to accepting me for the study, I had to have a blood test. I sat down with a very unpleasant nurse. She took what appeared to be a pen nib and tried to prick my finger—no blood came out, so she moved on to finger number two... same result. Eventually, she went through all my fingers and none of them yielded enough blood. She put a small bandage on each very sore finger and thanked me for trying to sign up for the experiment. I asked if I would get any payment for trying. She looked up at me and said, "Of course not." I walked out of the lab with ten bandaged fingers and...

no money. I thought about going to the university and taking a Rorschach test to see if the psychology students could discern whether or not I was deeply depressed.

I needed the $50 down payment that I *thought* had been promised for trying to participate in the drug study that didn't work out, so... it was time to go to the well, i.e. Brigham and Women's Hospital. They were so reliable; they coveted me; I had A+ blood and though it isn't very rare, it is rare enough that whenever they scheduled an open-heart operation with an A+ patient, I would get a call and, they would pay me $50 on the spot—give the blood, get the money. Every six weeks, I would be eligible to give blood, however, if they had an urgent need for my blood, they would overlook the six-week requirement. I once gave blood only three weeks after having made a donation. So, in my desperation, I decided to call the hospital and see if they might need a good dose of A+ blood.

I got through to a receptionist and I asked if they needed some A+ blood. She said they didn't accept call-ins and they would call me. I said, "Look, I heard they need some A+ blood right now," so I said, "Would you please ask the doctor? This might be an emergency." She complied and returned to the phone and said, "Would you be able to stop by within the next hour?" "Yes," I said, "I will be there in less than an hour."

As a short sidebar to my story, it is important to note that I am very squeamish about seeing blood—I go faint and have even passed out at the sight of blood. Therefore, becoming a blood donor was a very very big deal for me. Before I became a paid donor, I met with the Brigham and Women's staff about the blood-donating procedure and they walked me through the process and convinced me that I would never have to see any blood. OK… I agreed. They wanted A+ blood, and I wanted the money.

The procedure worked just fine. I'd lie down on a table, look to the left, close my eyes, and let them put the needle in my right arm, and, as promised, they put adhesive tape on the needle so it couldn't slip out—good so far. At the end of the procedure, they would remove the tape and the needle from my arm—my eyes remained closed. And then they would seal the deal. They'd place a check for $50 right on my chest and tell me to open my eyes. Wow! No blood in sight and money in my hands—and then they would give me a small glass of very cold orange juice. Life was good, the money was good, so good in fact, that I visited the hospital about 8 to 10 times a year for several years. I thought of myself as a professional… Donor.

Now back to the story. I rushed to the hospital and went right to the blood donation department. The nurse had me lie down on the table, I turned to the left and offered my right arm. She inserted the needle, and… walked away without placing the tape on the needle. I called out, "Nurse, nurse!" to no avail, she was out of earshot. I was having a panic attack—I could barely breathe — I could envision the needle popping out of my arm and blood spurting all over the lab. *Breathe deep breathe slowly*," I kept repeating to myself… "Everything will be fine."

But everything wasn't fine. Yes, the nurse removed the needle without a problem, but, there was no check on my chest—where was the goddamn check? More panic. The nurse said that the "new procedure" was to give me a chit that I could redeem at the bursar's desk in the main atrium of the hospital. *Breathe deep breathe slowly.* So I asked, "Where is my orange juice?" The nurse said that a new doctor had determined that the juice was unnecessary. "What, what are you doing to me?" I asked, and received... a blank stare, and then the reply, "Here is your chit, and by the way, you will have to accept the new procedures."

I was faint, I was nauseous, I grasped my chit and staggered to the hospital's large domed atrium. I entered from the left and I could see the bursar's office on the far right side. I weaved toward the office where my chit would be honored. I made it to the very center of the dome, and... I threw-up. I emptied my stomach right in the middle of the atrium. I suppose people were looking at me, but I didn't care in the least. The hospital had brought this mess on themselves. I did get a little bit of bile on my shoes, but that was of no concern to me. I now walked proudly to the bursar, who didn't seem concerned about my accident, and I handed her my chit. She gave me fifty dollars.

I turned and looked at the atrium as I was leaving. I saw the janitors dealing with the mess on the floor. I saw patients and staff pretending not to notice as they calmly avoided the area under the dome.

I reached in my pocket and held fast... to the hard-earned blood money. I knew... I would never sell, or give, blood again.

Island Beach

Dey be Mon
   And Womon—
Womon walk da beach, she say,
"Missy, dis scarf be for you,
Lady, dees beeds   you
   will look so fine.
Honey, you could do
   wit massage."

Mon   he stands in place,
   "I got da beech chair
   Da-umbrella   all day
   Two free beer…
     Wi-fi   yeah
   I have."

And here in Paradise, it's tough
   Hawking to tourists, rich tourists.
Mon says,
   "Why dey don't just buy?
   Den I go home."

I feel
   Like I should buy   something—
I don't, but I do…
Talk.
I tell them stories of snow… three feet high,
Temperatures—minus ten degrees!

They are amazed—
They shake their heads
    "Sorry, Mon," they say
        "We gawn stay—
        Have da sky be blue
        All day   warm
        Da ocean...
    Always der...

Sorry, Mon."

I Am...

1. A man conflicted at dawn
2. A brother of a brother who is dying
3. A person with guilt, that he will live on
4. A man who knows each day is a gift
5. A man with a brother who will have none of this
6. A man who wonders where his brother's tomorrows
   have gone
7. A man with a burden and joy... to carry on
8. A man with tomorrow and more perhaps
9. A man who waits for his song   to pass.

On Peggy's Porch

The last time I saw Logan
    It was on a summer's night,
    A little past midnight,
And hours before a new day began.

I was driving down Joe English Hill,
    And on my right, below a dimly lit light—
    Logan and Peggy both in plain sight
Were kissing and hugging as teenagers will.

I too had been on Peggy's porch
    In truth, it seemed not long ago,
    Not caring who might, or might not know,
That I was the one who carried a torch,

    For Peggy there on Peggy's porch.

If

If I sat on the beach
    from noon until four
Would a book be my companion?
Would I read it to the end?

If I sat at the beach
    from noon until four
Would I watch the bathers walking by?
Would I try and guess their ages?

If I sat at the beach
    from noon until four
Would I wiggle my toes in the sand?
Might I leave footprints on the shore?

If I sat on the beach
    from noon until four
Would I gaze upon the cloudless sky?
Would it be bluer than blue?

If I sat at the beach
    from noon until four
Would I watch the boats go sailing by?
Might I wonder where they're bound?

If I sat at the beach
    from noon until four
What would keep me there?
    the sun
    the sky
    the sand
    the salty air
The sea… is calling me.

If

When you were fourteen months old,
I was born,
Just think...
If I'd never been born,
I'd never have known you.
If I'd never known you
I'd never have loved you.
If I'd never loved you,
I'd never miss you.
But...
I did.
And I do.
And I will.

If

If I give you what you want
What will you ask of me?
If you give me what I need
You will set my heart free.

If I never stop crying for you
What will you think of me?
If you comfort me in my sadness
You will set my heart free.

If I talk to you sincerely
What would you say and do
     when I tell you that I miss you?
Would you answer me sincerely?
Tell me... "I miss you too."

— Victoria Forsyth

I was Phaedrus...

    & Phaedra was me—
we lived
    the fullness   of joy
    & the fullness of pain,

but Phaedra never understood...
never understood   my pain.

    Phaedrus remembers
love so intense—
    he was afraid—
afraid as he left his body
    that he might unite
    with her spirit   become
the oneness that was
    their love.

and he feared
    for his corporeal being

lying   soulless   on the bed.

Phaedrus... remembers

Leaving

For three months he's known
    Death —
    was standing by the door,
Not like being shot, or
Dropping to the floor
Because your heart...
    Just quit.

No, he was able to plan
Accounts and amounts
Of money to move
    From here to there
Bills got paid plans were laid
    For a celebration of life.

The Reaper now
Has entered the room
He is teasing the ghost
From a wizened body—
A body too weak
    To retain its soul.

There is the smell...
Of the Reaper   and
The aura of the dying
That only the living...
    Can see.
It is time to leave.

    Goodbye.

Madison Square in May

A nanny pushes a leather pram
    Unnoticed by an artful man
Plein air painting   with paints gathered
    From who knows where—
Dogs go sniffing here and there

Burly guys on parade in muscle shirts
    Leggy girls wiggle in mini-skirts
Kousa and roses all abloom
    Gather warmth on a sun-blessed day
Two days on   in the month of May.

Recession

Autumn
    like a freight train
    rolls   over green hills
Pearly Everlasting
    (but not the summer)
flying
    the colors of battle
September
    blowing in   on a blue sky
            —Everyone needs a job—

She
    on a balance beam
    beaming at baby
    chewing her chemistry—
    pharmaceutically… speaking
& me
    well my fingers need nails
    like banks need money
& September needs rain.

six seconds
    a mile
third of a day
New York to LA
left coast Santa Monica
skate babes and guys
sweating   for joy   can
you believe it?
others   on the pier fishing
… for supper.

wind off the south seas
& sun only
8 minutes away—
    (if the payroll
    wasn't in the bank
    I'd still   warm my ass in the sun
    —drink my wine
    lie   on Gaviota
    stroking
        your pubic mound
        under cotton sheets
    twisting   in the warm breezes
    landed at last)

overhead   those fucking gulls
    move with a grace
    that in flight   redeems
    with beauty
the beggary nastiness
    screeching & farting
of their day to day   life.

—Santa Inez
the padre instructed
    the Chumash on playing…
    the fucking tuba for Christ
    sakes   I saw them   etched—
    in pen and ink—
the tuba fife and drum
    Amerind band.

Ojai to Ventucopa
    new weather
    new sites
Tehachapi crows

cawing in the live oaks
hawks circling   waiting for roadkill
    we move
    through our dreams dragging
    family and friends
    (if she'd just
    put her hand in my lap)
desert sun
drying my skin drying my soul
(i'd be a happy man.)

Barstow baking in CA sun…
i'm considering
    bowling a string
    when the so young thing
    in crotch-tight jeans
    & a fistful of keys, asks…
"can i help you?"
"*well, maybe,*" i'm thinking   but She after peeing
wants to go
so no   oh no bowling today…

let's go watch the trains
    struggle to Tchachapi, or
follow them down to Apple Valley
for a plate of steamed burritos —
i want
to push the big car
get to 100 or more — well,
i backed off at 88
    as She
    worked the ruby stone file
    on nails that i could use.

i talked
to baby this morning   told him
i ravished his mother
to start the day   (yes,
he's only a baby   but he has to know
who is the boss… that would be… me.)

arms in the air
    Joshua trees
breeze in the desert.
        blowing the smog
        that followed I-10
        east from LA and
    it cuddles   the mountains
        the jumbo rocks   high desert forests
        yucca & black bush.

unsaved
deserts are trailored
bounded   by rusting cars and washing machines
fenced   by found stones painted   white
guarded by   dogs starving that bite
from hunger   and not conviction
and I drift
on east winds that
return the smog
home to LA
summoning
stars like crystals
in the desert night-
and from San Jacinto
i'm a pretend god as i survey
    this sparkling world
        before my feet   that is mine.

my son on the phone
now 6 months old…
unspeaking… he's pissed
at day-away parents-
"but Sonny we have
bags of trinkets, and
more than that   we will have time,"
and on the day of coming home
San Jacinto
is lost in white clouds… palms
and blue skies.

Shinto Gateway

Passing
From the mundane
   To the sacred
'Through a Torii
   Welcoming all.

I pull on a rope
   To ring the bell
   That awakens the Kami—
I bow twice   I clap
   My hands twice
I call upon all ancestors,
   Known and unknown—
I tell them   How I am,
   What I do.
I thank them
   For making the path

   That brought me…

To my soul.

I clap again, I bow—
   I leave…

November

Naked now the trees, stark without their leaves
Not one to wave in a wintery breeze—
The season affronts my copse of trees
And easy days are nowhere to be found
They've moved on to a warmer town
Leaving a sadness in the so-crisp air
Urging the bear to his wintertime lair
There to dream of a coming green season,
Berries red ripe, new life so pleasing.

The days will be short with unyielding snow
And the flora and fauna wisely know
To huddle and cuddle just to survive
Their only goal is to remain alive.

November can be a prelude to spring
A dream of a season that soon will bring
Weary winter dreamers a fresh new start
Red ripe with berries   a new life apart.

On Leaving My Love Behind

Pray for me my dear
Before this coming night
It is not death I fear

My life's path was always clear
I'll miss your face at dawn's first light
Pray for me my dear

What sounds I'll no longer hear
On my endless flight through endless night
It is not death I fear

The touch of your hand as you draw near
That always allays unneeded fright
Pray for me my dear

Can eternity ever be so dear
As loving you for just one night?
It is not death I fear.

I'll leave with only a single tear
A lifeless body in the dead of night
Pray for me my dear
It is not death I fear.

Alunizaron

> *Ensconced in a spa tub*
> *Gazing*
> *Above   peering*
> *Through coconut   palms*
> *Whiskey with ice in hand*
> *Back-lit by a cloudless dusk-blue sky*
> *And a gibbous moon searching*
> *For fulfillment,   I ponder*
> *Where and with whom*
> *Will we dine tonight?*

I didn't always think like that.

It wasn't always a life lived on the edge of luxury—there were the '50s and fistfights for any reason or none, black leather jackets, engineer boots, swagger, Ike, the military-industrial complex, boosted cars, switchblades, peg-pants, duck-ass hairdos, girls were everywhere in swing dresses, tight jeans and short-shorts, TVs, new car designs every year, grease and "cool" and the beginnings of "Beat." We knew, as a country, we were heading somewhere, probably somewhere better—a new decade was coming—the '60s.

And 1960 was going to be a big year for me—I would turn 16 in July of 1960, and that meant that I could get my driver's license. Getting a license was more of a big deal to me than most other teenagers, and that was because one of the nuns who had taught me in grammar school shared the insight that the world would end in

1960 (i.e., the year that the Pope could open the letter given by our Lady of Fatima to the three Portuguese children—the letter to be opened in 1960 — obviously, would say, "Sorry boys and girls, but it is time to end this interlude called 'Living on Earth.'") It's easy to Monday-morning quarterback the nun's pronouncement, but at the time I was only ten-years-old and nuns were, so I had been instructed... infallible. I immediately asked the nun if the world would end at the beginning of 1960, or nearer to the end. She told me, "It would end just after Christmas." "Whew!" I would have almost six months to drive a car before being called home to Heaven.

The big year rolled around, I got my license and I had full access to my father's 1954 Hillman Minx wagon as long as I delivered groceries to spinsters, mad cat women and the occasional normal family—seemed like a fair deal to me. I delivered orders from 3:30 PM to 6 PM and then... the Hillman Minx, stick-shift on the floor (how cool was that?) wagon was mine for the rest of the night. FREEDOM, I'm talking about real freedom! There were only a few other boys in the entire high school who had full access to a vehicle every night of the week.

My freedom had two important consequences, a.) I became... popular—classmates sought me out, and b.) Schoolwork suffered even more than it had before. My grades, which were poor to begin with,... plummeted. I convinced myself that good grades didn't really matter. I had plenty of money for a 16-year-old teenager. I had two paper routes, a morning route and a Sunday route, a grocery delivery job after school, and a full day of work at my father's store on Saturday. As Alfred E. Neuman always said, "What me worry?"

During the autumn of 1960, politics dominated the news, and even general family discussions revolved around the coming election. A youngish Senator, a Catholic, from Massachusetts was running against Richard Nixon for the Presidency, and since I was in a Catholic High School, the election became a very big deal. My mother was infatuated with Kennedy; my father liked him, my delivery customers wanted to talk about him—"What did I think?" they asked. Not wanting to appear stupid, and since my curiosity was piqued, I began to watch the news on TV, generally, the late-night news.

It all came together on the evening of Saturday, November 5th, and the early morning hours of Sunday, Nov 6th, 1960. Senator Jack Kennedy was coming to Waterbury, Connecticut. His plane was going to land in Strafford, CT and then his motorcade would follow Route 8 along the Naugatuck River passing through towns like Shelton, Derby, Ansonia, Seymour, Beacon Falls, Naugatuck, Union City and ending the procession in Waterbury. There were thousands of people in every town lining the route cheering and waving flags—it was chilly, it was raining and people, mostly Catholics, were there to declare their allegiance to the first great Catholic hope since Al Smith who ran for President in 1928. (It was probably a good thing that he lost because the Great Depression started in 1929.)

Kennedy didn't get to Waterbury until almost 1 AM. The crowd had been waiting and would have waited all night. Word spread electrically through the crowd— Kennedy had arrived at the Roger Smith Hotel—he would be speaking from a second-floor balcony that overlooked the Waterbury Green. The gathering was estimated at over 50,000 in a city of only 100,000 people. And they were cheering in anticipation, unlike anything I had ever seen. I had seen Yankee Stadium explode after a Mickey Mantle home run, but the spectators were cheering for the event, i.e. the home run, more than they were cheering for Mantle. Here they were cheering totally for the person. He was electric.

I was with my girlfriend, Peggy, and she was as excited as a human being could get and not explode. There aren't words to describe the exuberance of the throng as he stepped on to the balcony. **KENNEDY KENNEDY KENNEDY** shouts echoed off the buildings. I knew how I felt and I remember wondering how it must feel to be on the receiving end of such adulation.

And then he spoke—

"The cause of America is the cause of all Mankind… If we fail here, if we drift, if we lie at anchor, if we don't provide an example of what freedom can do in the 1960s, then we will have betrayed not only ourselves and our destiny, but all those who desire to be free."

And then paraphrasing Lincoln, he said, **"We see the storm coming and we know His hand is in it. But if He has a place for me, I believe that we are ready. Thank you."**

The people were cheering, crying, it was as if Jesus had come to Town. I knew I believed. Yes, goddammit—I would do better—I would put myself in a position to be a leader. And that is exactly what I did.

I began to study—chemistry, physics, trigonometry, language—anything they could throw at me for the last half of my junior and all of my senior year. I still worked and had the Hillman, but most nights, I was at home studying and trying to catch up with the other students who had been studying all these many years. Kennedy's words stuck with me and I was going to be ready for… **"the storm coming."** I was going to be a part of…**"Providing an example of what freedom can do."**

I lived up to and surpassed my goals—I was admitted to Northeastern University's College of Engineering. Wow! Two years ago I was adrift and now, in September of 1962, I'm in my dorm room studying engineering with some really smart people. And then, after I had only been at Northeastern for about a week, I heard on the radio that JFK went to Houston and said…*"We choose to go to the moon in this decade… because that challenge is one that we are willing to accept, one that we are unwilling to postpone…"* Yes, yes, and yes—I knew the country was moving toward greatness. I was congratulating myself for having understood the Kennedy vision and for having taken the steps necessary to be in a position to participate in greatness.

However, by October 14th, just six weeks later, there was news—Soviet nuclear missiles were in Cuba. The world was about to change.

On October 16th, Kennedy talked about a blockade of all Soviet ships headed to Cuba. Khrushchev responded and said that a blockade would be… **"a violation of freedom to use international waters and international air space and is an act of aggression."**

Kennedy answers… **"It is the policy of this nation to regard any nuclear weapon launched against any city in the Western Hemisphere as an attack by the Soviet Union requiring a full retaliatory response by the US on the Soviet Union."**

Every night my roommates and I would listen to Jerry Williams on Boston radio discuss the *storm coming*. Could nuclear war be averted? Did Khruschev view Kennedy as weak? Were we in the midst of a global game of chicken? Might there be a preemptive strike? Would Boston be a target? The '60s weren't going in the direction I had anticipated. Could the nun have been right about the end of the world? Maybe she was just off by two years? If you didn't live during those times, you will be unable to grasp the innate fear of nuclear war, any more than I could understand the bombing of London during WWII.

It all came to a head on the 24th. Kennedy called the action a quarantine instead of a blockade. Khruschev responded that… **"it is an act of aggression and Soviet ships will be instructed to ignore the blockade."**

On the 25th, Kennedy said… **"the weapons in Cuba are offensive weapons and will not be allowed near our border."** Surprisingly, fourteen Russian ships turned around. The ships that continued toward Cuba were boarded and since they didn't have weapons, they were allowed to continue to Cuba.

On the 27th, Robert Kennedy and Anatoly Dobrynin met and struck a deal. Russia agreed to remove the missiles from Cuba and the US promised not to invade the Island. There was also a "side-deal" whereby the US would remove nuclear missiles from Turkey and Italy. Crisis averted.

Saturday the 27th of October, 1962 is considered *"**the most dangerous day in the History of Mankind.**"* I was pondering greatness for the world... not annihilation.

Now that the crisis was averted, I could get back to work—and I did. If I wasn't working at school, I was at my Co-op job.

I remember having a rare free Friday afternoon on November 22nd, 1963. I took the "T" from Northeastern to Arlington Station and exited before the normal Boylston stop so that I could walk across the Boston Public Garden and then down Charles Street to my apartment on West Cedar Street. It was a beautiful New England, Indian Summer day.

I crossed Boylston Street and entered the Gardens—I inhaled a deep breath of fresh late autumn air, and all felt right with the world. And then I noticed people running, yelling, crying—what was going on? A young student ran up to me and said, Kennedy had been shot— Jesus Christ, I thought, this simply can't be. I continued walking in a state of disbelief—watching people screaming, crying, and by the time I got to Charles Street, people were yelling that Kennedy was pronounced... dead. *How can that possibly be? For fuck's sakes every time things seem to be going well, something really terrible happens. I refused to believe... that JFK was dead.*

Whether I believed it or not, he was dead. On the radio... commentators, "at 12:30 PM in Dallas— shots rang out, president was hit, raced to hospital, 30 minutes later, pronounced dead, LBJ sworn in on the jet back to DC, a nation in shock, Saturday... autopsy, Sunday lies in state at the Capitol Rotunda, Monday... funeral procession through DC, Mass at Saint Matthew, procession to Arlington Cemetery, 3:50 PM, Monday, November 25th... burial."

My roommates and I felt that we had to be a part of this terrible moment in History. Three women friends from a nearby Boston College wanted to come with us on our planned pilgrimage to DC. One of my roommates had a large station wagon that could hold the six of us. One of the women who wanted to make the trip... was Peggy. She had been with me when Kennedy came to Waterbury just three years previous... *Could it have been only three years? So much had happened to the Country in those three years—my life had metamorphosed—from caterpillar to butterfly.*

And there we were on Monday, November 25th, 1963 standing on Pennsylvania Avenue—the six of us, after having driven all night, we could but stand and witness six white horses pulling a flag-draped coffin on a Civil War era caisson, followed by Black Jack, the riderless horse with black, calvary boots facing backward.

As the procession passed, the crowd began to disperse—there was nothing more that could be done. We turned and it seemed like we were turning our backs on our dreams.

We had time to think about it during our 8-hour drive back to Boston... after all, we would have class on Tuesday, a half-day on Wednesday and then head home for Thanksgiving.

The general malaise and melancholy lingered—many of the young people felt that the assassination had been directed at them, and then things spiraled out of control— conspiracy theories abounded—who was Jack Ruby and how was he able to get so close to Lee Harvey Oswald? How many shooters were there? What about the grassy knoll? Does anyone really like LBJ? Will he escalate the conflict in Vietnam?

The next few years were... tedious—problems would not go away. Vietnam got worse, thousands of additional troops each week, college protests expanded as the war expanded, and in the background, the Civil Rights Movement was coming to a boil. My roommates and I made two or three trips to DC to participate in the bigger rallies, the ones where Martin Luther King drew huge crowds, and then war protesters and Civil Rights activists began to unite their causes. LBJ did get the Civil Rights Act passed, but the war hawks had his ear and body bags were returning from Vietnam at an alarming rate. Blacks were marching, students were marching, everybody was mad about something. By 1967 Eugene McCarthy had become the anti-war candidate and was going to challenge LBJ in the 1968 election. Much of the anti-war movement had morphed into the "Hippie" movement... "Turn on, tune in, drop out." ("If you're going to San Francisco / be sure to wear some flowers in your hair...") It was the year to leave it all behind and hang in San Francisco. I made the pilgrimage during the summer of '67 and spent a couple of days at Haight-Ashbury, observing—I wasn't a hippie. I did have longish hair and I would enjoy a marijuana treat now and then, but it was a small part of my life. Based on my observations, I came to the conclusion that the Hippie lifestyle was a dead end. So, in the late Fall of '67, when I was working on my Master's Degree in Engineering, I decided to use the small amount of free time available to me, to work for the expected candidacy of Eugene McCarthy.

Here we are in 1968—I'm working on my Master's Degree, running to NH to do whatever I'm asked to do by the McCarthy Campaign and then on March 12th, primary day, I drove to Manchester, NH and my job was to take voters to the polls. Anyone needing a ride would call the office, and I would go and take them to the appropriate polling location. After the polls closed, I ate supper and then went to the Sheraton Bedford to watch the results come in. It was incredibly exciting to see the number of votes that were going to McCarthy. The gathered throng of young supporters had some crazy hope that he could pull it out. He didn't, but he did get 42% of the vote against an incumbent President. LBJ realized that the Country was distressed about the Vietnam War, and on March 31st he announced... "I will neither seek nor accept... the Democratic nomination."

McCarthy's followers were ecstatic. However, Robert Kennedy, once LBJ was out of the race, decided to enter the remaining primaries. McCarthy's followers were displeased that Kennedy would enter the race after McCarthy had done all the heavy lifting. *But, in our hearts we knew...* Bobby was the heir to the throne.

If you are following the timeline, you will have noticed that there were many depressing downturns through these turbulent years, but, there would always be some little glimmer of hope for a better day. The Space Program was moving along, but it was still a long way from the JFK promise to land a man on the moon by the end of the decade. LBJ had decided not to run and that offered hope for an end to the Vietnam War.

I was pondering all these ups and downs and thinking that perhaps the Country had turned the corner. Maybe there will be better days ahead. It was just after supper on April 4th, 1968, only five days after LBJ had given the peace movement a sliver of hope by stating that he would not run for President. I poured myself a well-earned drink after a long day in the Hydraulics Lab. I sat back, turned on the TV… and… I could have passed out. Martin Luther King had just been assassinated. I had no words, just emptiness and then they quoted some parts of the speech King had given the previous night to a group of followers in Memphis.

"We've got some difficult days ahead, but it doesn't matter to me now, because I've been to the mountaintop…"… "and I've seen the Promised Land…"… "and I'm happy tonight. I'm not worried about anything. I'm not fearing any man. My eyes have seen the glory of the coming of the Lord."
Maybe King had a premonition about impending death. But his death wasn't going to make things better, at least initially, it was going to set cities afire. Was this what JFK meant when he paraphrased Lincoln about the **"coming storm?"**

The whole country was "sick." I had barely escaped the Boston Race Riots that happened on June 2, 1967, and now it seemed almost certain that racial issues combined with the ever more depressing news from Vietnam would have the Country in turmoil for the foreseeable future. Well, there was one more hope and that would be Robert Kennedy. I was reluctant to drop my support for McCarthy, but, there was only one person who had a chance to make things right in our troubled country... *The Heir.*

I watched the news about the upcoming primaries. Kennedy was gaining ground, but Hubert Humphrey, who had also entered the presidential race after the LBJ announcement, was the favorite of the local pols and was collecting delegates in non-primary states. Humphrey's strategy of avoiding the primaries became a real issue with younger and anti-war voters—they saw Humphrey as someone who would continue the war. By May, RFK was becoming a force to be reckoned with—he won primaries in Indiana and Nebraska but then lost to McCarthy in Oregon on May 28th. That loss in Oregon set up the big night of June 4th when South Dakota and California would decide the winner of their primaries. As it turned out, Kennedy won both South Dakota and California on June 4th. I went to bed that night believing that RFK would be hard to stop.

When I awoke on June 5th—everyone's worst nightmare had come true. Robert Kennedy had been shot—not dead, but the implications were that even if he survived, he would not be... viable. "**NOT AGAIN NOT AGAIN**," Americans were thinking and saying. June 5th became known as "the day lost in history."

Everyone knew that whether RFK lived or died, any chance at redemption was… over.

When I awoke on June 6th, I turned on the TV and there was Frank Mankiewicz:

"I have a short announcement to read, which I will read at this time. Senator Robert Francis Kennedy died at 1:14 AM, June 6, 1968. With Senator Kennedy at the time of his death were his wife Ethel, his sisters Mrs. Stephen Smith, Mrs. Patricia Lawford, his brother-in-law Mr. Stephen Smith and his sister-in-law Mrs. John F. Kennedy. He was 42 years old. Thank you."

"NOT AGAIN NOT AGAIN NOT AGAIN NOT AGAIN NOT AGAIN NOT AGAIN NOT…"

The day lost in history, June 5th was a day in limbo—reality returned on June 6th—if you remember RFK was at the center of "the most dangerous day in the history of mankind, 10/27/ 62," and here he was at the center of "the day lost in history, June 5th,1968."

Acceptance acceptance acceptance. All we could do was to sit back and watch the rest of the year play itself out—riots in the cities, riots at the Democratic Convention when Hubert Humphrey was chosen by the politicians, and finally a victory by Richard Nixon over Humphrey. (As depressed as McCarthy and Kennedy's followers were, it was ironic that Nixon got the Country out of the war, started the EPA and made inroads to China.) I had an opportunity to go to Venezuela and I decided to take it. In my mind, there was nothing I could do in the US. Perhaps I could accomplish something in another country, or at least get a new perspective on the world.

I settled in easily to the slower pace of life in Venezuela, my name translated to Roberto Cruz, and within a few months, I was beginning to feel like a local. The US news always seemed secondary to what was happening in my life, other than the news about the space program. Sometimes those JFK words… **"We choose to go to the moon in this decade…"** would pop into my head and I would wonder if it was really going to happen. Of course, none of my Venezuela friends gave it any credibility so I would never bring it up in conversation.

Time passed with a certain rhythm in Cumana, Sucre, Venezuela. My Spanish kept improving and I was accomplishing what I considered important work by extending water lines to barrios that had been without water and getting the City to undertake other civic projects which I would design and oversee.

And then, on Sunday afternoon, July 20th, 1969, I was visiting a friend who lived at the end of a peninsula in a house that was right on the ocean. His house was the very last house and to reach it I had to drive my motorcycle through a very poor barrio. The houses were of *bahareque* construction, meaning they were built from mud or clay with pieces of wood and/or bamboo for reinforcement. Dogs and cats ran wild and naked children played in roadside ditches. The children ran in and out of houses without any concern as to whether or not it was their house. There were also other animals like pigs and goats wandering around and chickens and roosters were as common as sparrows.

My friend's house didn't have a working TV, so I walked to one of the barrio houses that had an old Philco console TV sitting in the entry room. I had met the woman before and I asked if I could watch the TV because they were going to show the moon landing. She rolled her eyes, nodded her head, yes, and returned to the kitchen.

In addition to the TV, there was one Naugahyde-clad love-chair and a side table with a small lamp. The front door was kept open and children could run through the main room, into the kitchen, and then outside again to play in the mud and rubbish. I sat down with a tall rum and coke that I had brought with me. I turned on the TV and the expected landing was hosted by Renny Ottolina, host of the nationally popular, "El Show de Renny." Renny was some excited, they were getting a direct feed from the US—Renny would translate English into Spanish. It was exciting as the Lander approached the moon. And then Renny screamed **"Alunizaron Alunizaron." (they have landed on the moon.)** And as he spoke, a 300-pound sow walked in the front door, gave me not a look, went to the kitchen and exited through the back door, then a couple of naked kids ran through the room, I don't think they even saw me.

That is how the decade of the '60s ended for me—sitting on a Naugahyde sofa, (remember it all started with the Kennedy motorcade coming up the Naugatuck Valley and passing the Naugatuck Chemical Plant where they made the world-famous... Naugahyde) drinking my rum and coke, listening to Renny shouting **"Alunizaron" and knowing that no one, and I mean no one in Venezuela, believed the US went to the**

moon. They all knew that the landing was filmed in Arizona.

JFK's promise was fulfilled. Was the tumult of the '60s worth it? Or did it just have to be?

Alunizaron!

Note - On the night of July 18th, 1969, while Apollo 11 was en route to the moon, Ted Kennedy… drove off the Chappaquiddick Bridge in Hyannis, Massachusetts.

And What of the Condo at Brighton Beach

In the crisp of a Sunday morning
On a bus in the opposing lane
Pushing through the grey-pink fog-off-the-moor
Whilst on my way to London
My peace was vexed by the beep
Of an incoming tweet.
Alright alright I silenced the beep
And glanced at the tweet...

"Uncle Mick died... just last night."

Christ-on-a-bike and Bloody Hell
The cheeky sod
Left the wife and kids to take the piss,
And scared the bejesus
Out of friends yet alive.

And what of the condo on Brighton Beach?
That was to be, now not to be
His refuge by the sea.

If there is something you would like to do,
Seize the day, old-chap
Tomorrow may, or may never... be.

Death   like tomorrow
Brooks no care nor sorrow.

The Queen Opines on Keats and Coleridge

It was pleasant crossing The Pond,
New York to Southampton   and on
By bus to London and
    all the sounds   the sites & smells   trams & prams
    all black cabs the *Shard*   the eye   the Palace, and
Big Ben   Yes, we are pleased to be back.

Because of my stature and renown, I was granted
The fewest of minutes   with the elderly Queen.
And I told good Queen Mother   that a friend
Of mine was contrasting
The philosophes of two English poets,
And that would be Keats and Coleridge.

And the Queen said to me, "I hope that your friend
Isn't taken   with that youngster Keats—Christ on a
    bike
He was a cheeky, twat-faced sod   a true
Wanker and a bumptious tosser."
So I said, "Dear Queen, might you opine
For the sake of mine and my dear friend
upon the manly Coleridge?"
The Queen said, "Now there was a manly man,
Which is not to say that he didn't overspend
    his time at the local Apothecary, however
    you need to know that he wouldn't,
    be taking the piss from no one   no Dearee
    he would tell those rat-arsed, poncy,
    wankers from Crawley
    A thing-a-two… unlike that young poofter Keats."

I thanked the Queen for her candor—
Her thoughts I would pass to my friend.
And then, I respectfully asked her, "My dear and
    endearing Queen
are your thoughts and opinions infallible,
When shared with a Cross-Pond wanker?"
"Of course they are, young man," she said,
"And I am surprised you had to ask."
"Lo siento mucho," I said to the Queen.
"Aceptado mi joven," she said.

She is bi-lingual...   it would seem.

Hosanna *(and goodbye)*

When Jesus comes to London
On a slow-moving barge,
He'll sail up the Thames
Like a Regent in charge
Who knows all the righteous, and
Knows all their names

From noon until sundown
He'll greet all believers
Wave to Holy achievers —
Sign autographs   pose
A few selfies for those
Who troubled to drive into Town

He'll stop at Cathedral Saint Paul
Look upon the masses and ponder the FALL
And timing when all...

No longer will be.

Wilbur and the Therapist

Wilbur pined for a tryst
With the oh so sensual,
Bibliotherapist

Sure, he loved books
As many a man might
Although it was her looks —
Her alluring looks
And grace when speaking of books
That brought on an ache
When he decided to speak
And as he opened his mouth…
The Ship's Captain spake…
Over the intercom, calm
Yet insistent he addressed
His need for the therapist
So alas poor Wilbur
Saw an opportunity missed
To conjugate with…
The bibliotherapist

The Least of Life

The least of life, the smallest of the small
naught but an unmarried RNA Strand
casting its shadow and spreading a pall

not over just my life, but the lives of all
who know its power and understand
the least of life, the smallest of the small

can stride like a giant ten feet tall
gathering death in locals unplanned
casting its shadow and spreading a pall.

Upon what or whom shall I call?
Upon what altar shall I stand?
and implore the least of life, the smallest of the small,

to show small mercy on what may befall
My life confronted by a now-married *Strand*,
casting its shadow, and spreading a pall.

This virus may soon… rule over all.
No longer atop creation, as planned,
I Hail, *Least of Life, the Smallest of the Small…*
Casting its shadow, and spreading a pall.

*Theater in the Time of Covid-19**

Algernon and Gwen
Live the country life in coastal Maine
Though they know more
Of New York City than most
That call it home.

Algy, "call me Ernest," and
Gwendolyn, "call me Gwen,"
Toil in flowered gardens,
Attend a Book Club event or two, and
Do a decent docent job
At the in-town tourist zoo.

Once a month like moon-crazed
Wolves they'd board a City-bound bus—
Six hours later like mice
Approaching the end of a maze
Their hearts would race, their
Spirits uplift upon seeing the lights
And planning three nights
In the place they called... Civilization.

Ernest, I call him Ernie, and
His brilliant wife Gwen   upon
Returning from Civilization
Would regale me with tales of the Broadway Theater.
The year before the virus (Ernie would say, "Struck.")
There were play revivals like "Rose Tattoo,"
and "All My Sons." And two wondrous new plays,
"To Kill a Mockingbird," and "Network."

"Has there ever been, or
Will there ever be?" Ernest asked of me,
"A year so full, that made our life so full
as the year before the flu?"

Now two years beyond the flu,
The pandemic loiters on crowded corners
Unwilling to be forgotten.   Gwen and Ernie
now only visit but once a year
The place that fed the soul,
Expanded the mind and
Let them leave the countryside
Behind.

The City now is dull and distanced -
Playgoers, masked, sit in every fourth row,
Restaurant patrons
Occupy every third table—
"Sure it costs more, and
We have more room," Gwen said,
"And if we wanted solace and ample space,
Then this
Would be the place."

"It's a whole new world," Ernest
Muttered - "not the place it used to be
And not the place for me."

"Corona is King," Queen Gwendolyn said,
"15,000 dance on the head of a pin—
they're a life-form less than life, you know,
Needful of a host in order to grow."

And now depressed, old Algy said,
"The virus has won, Civilization... undone.

Come along Gwen, we've flowers to tend
... our lives to amend."

  * The names of the characters are roughly based on
those in the play, "The Importance of Being Earnest," by
Oscar Wilde.

I can do this...

1. I was in the savanna, hiding in the tall grass, spear honed and ready, waiting for a lost or lonesome ibex—too much thinkin', not enough smellin', and the hyenas found me, afore I found my prey.
2. I was there at Jericho on a sunny autumn day, I was standing on the wall just looking at a puffy white cloud, and then came Joshua and a thousand ram horns blaring—and I, along with the wall, we all came tumbling down.
3. On a morning in October in 79 AD, I left Herculaneum to visit my Mom in Pompei —no need to say more… it was a very bad day.
4. General George Custer was a leader and a man I was proud to ride beside on June the 25th of 1876. Our trackers had said that the Lakota Sioux were numbered in the hundreds, but on that day our lives yielded to thousands, and it was only my soul that left   the Battle of Little Big Horn.
5. It was at the second Battle of Ypres in April of '15—I survived the first gas attack but not the bullet barrage that followed—"In Flanders Fields, the Poppies Grow," —I know… I have watched them from below.
6. On a Monday morning, just after 8 AM, on August the 6th of '45, I was walking by the Ota River and I heard an overhead hum… perhaps a plane and yes, it was. The Enola Gay had found its way to Hiroshima—then "Little Boy" jumped from the plane. I watched the arc of his flight. *This doesn't look good,* I thought—and then a flash… then death. That was the quickest I had ever died.

7. I've been to many places and died so many times
    only to rise again and find the challenges of my
    new life on my endless trip through time. And
    now I'm on my sofa, isolated, quarantined; I visit
    my friends on Zoom, I have Netflix and Amazon
    Prime, my food is brought to my door. I live in a
    marvelous virtual world, though a bit like being
    in a zoo—I'm always looking out but can't go out.
    They tell me on TV… it will pass, the unseeable
    threat will be vanquished, I simply have to wait.

    I can do this—I've been asked to do much more , I
    can do this.

Hobson's Choice   by Robert A. Cruess

Setting:

Late 1960's.
A bar in a small Hudson River town in upstate New
York. There is a simple bar table with a red-checkered
tablecloth and two chairs center stage.

Characters: (three male actors)

> **Villeroy Jones** (Vic)— An 18-year-old, Black, senior
> in High School. A hard-working young adult planning
> for his future.
> **Pyotr Leknikov** (Pete)— A 20-year-old, White male
> of Russian descent with professional parents in their
> 60's. Pete is self-centered, egotistical, lazy, and always
> needs money. He is Vic's friend and is still in high
> school.
> **Mori**—the barkeep
> **Police Chief Harris**

> **Played by the same actor: Mori**—ordinary barkeep,
> wears a white apron.
> > **Police Chief Harris—**
> wears a police hat and a badge.

Production Notes:

Vic and Pete are dressed like typical teenagers—they
wear jeans, T-shirts and light-weight jackets. The
bartender is off stage and appears only when asked to
bring a beer. Similarly, the Police Chief is off stage and
enters only on cue.

At Rise:

*There is a small bar table with a red-checkered tablecloth
and two chairs. Vic and Pete enter from stage right, walk
over and sit at the table.*

Pete

Hey, Mori, bring us a coupla' Jennys, will ya?
This round's on you, Vic. I'm down to no money—just
put it on my tab.

Vic

You're the man with the big house, rich Mom, rich Dad,
new car, so why am I the bank for the beer? The gas? And
any other thing that you need but can't pay for?

Pete *(Mori places two bottles of beer on the table)*

C'mon man—what'd I owe ya? Maybe $200? You know
I'm good for it. Once old Mom and Dad get back from
wherever, I'll hit them up for the money.

Vic

Ya know Pete, you make your own problems. Your Mom
and Dad gave you plenty of money when they went on
vacation a few weeks ago. What'd you say? Five hundred
dollars? Then as soon as they left, you dropped $300 to a
hustler at the pool hall.

Pete

That boy from, what'd he say? Schoharie? Just like a
hungry fish, I grabbed the bait without thinkin'. He let
me win a coupla games then he upped the ante, started
playin' like Minnesota Fats—next thing ya know, he has
$300 a-mine. I know I ain't the smartest, but I didn't
think I was that dumb.

Vic

You're no college boy, but when you get to drinkin' and
thinkin'—you're done for, it's like a grammar school kid
against a Rensselaer cum laude.

Pete

How'd you know 'bout me losin' all that money to the
hustler?

Vic

I was there Pete—you'd been drinkin', so I tried to get
you to leave. You got pissed at me, so I left just as you lost
the last game and had to pay $300 to the backwoods
hustler.

Pete

So, I'm the guy with the rich parents and the new Camaro
and according to you, I cause all the problems but, I'll
admit, you do lend me money to get me through the dry
times. How is it that you keep your nose so clean and
always have some money in your pocket?

Vic

Nobody gives me money—I work a few nights at HoJo's
and I put most of my paycheck in my college account.

Pete

I suppose. Every now and then I think I should be doin'
what you're doin' —you know, workin', studying, saving
money and all that, but it never works out—I just go back
to being... me. If things get tight, I ask Mom and Dad for
more money.

Vic *(Vic and Pete drink some of their beer)*
Money is always an issue with you but I know you'll pay
me back.

What has me worried is what happened last Friday night.
I know I was some drunk when we left the bar and my
memory is a bit foggy—I remember us following behind
some old guy down Magnolia Street and you sayin', "Let's
roll the old geezer—see what he has for money?"

Pete

Are you sure I said, "Let's roll him?" Coulda been... you
said it.

Vic

Even drunk, I'd never say, "Let's roll 'em." I remember
you picked up a chunk of wood or something and gave the
poor bastard a whack in the head—the guy went down
like he'd been shot.

Pete

Well Vic, as I see it, you are confusin' the facts. It was you
that grabbed the 2x4 and gave the guy a baseball swing
across the head, then said, "Let's get outta here." You
scared me, man — never thought you would do
something like that.

Vic

C'mon Pete, I know what I did and didn't do. I did **not**
hit that guy. It was you. You said, "He'll be fine in the
mornin', just a small bump on his head."

Pete

You remember that Psych 101 course we took? There was
a mental thing where a person will "transfer" something
that they don't want to deal with mentally onto another
person. I think that's what's goin' on here... *transference.*

Vic

For Christ sakes Pete, you failed the fucking course and now you're babbling on as if you were a psychologist. First off you're scaring me and now I'm wondering if something did happen to the old guy?

Pete *(sits back, takes a deep breath and then a long swig from the bottle)*

Funny thing you bring that up, Vic, because I was going to talk to you about that very issue. There was no mention in the paper about the old guy getting rolled—he was a nobody, but, two days later... Son' bitch died. And that got the attention of the police.

Vic

Oh, Jesus Christ Pete, you said that you barely hit him—only got him dizzy, now you're telling me that he's dead and... we killed him.

Pete

I guess the guy was hit harder than you thought—you said he was OK and told me to follow you. I foolishly went along with you even though I was a little worried about the guy.

Vic

I think I'm gonna hurl.

Pete

Don't do it—but, back to the police—the dead guy got their attention and they began to investigate. They sent detectives up and down Magnolia and found somebody who had seen two young guys that night.

> **Vic**

I'm scared Pete! Are we in trouble?

> **Pete**

Let me finish. The police canvassed Magnolia Street and found a witness. The witness said he saw a big white guy with a smaller black guy walking away from a man who was laying on the ground. So the police went nosing around the high school—didn't take them long to call me. Who else is a big white guy who has a smaller black friend? The Chief himself handled the questioning— maybe because my Mom's a judge. Anyway, he was very thorough. He knew that I had nothing to do with what happened, but, just by being there, he said that I would be considered an accomplice. He also understood that I didn't go directly to the police because of my friendship with you.

> **Vic**

Pete, is this a joke? For Christ's sake, you know what happened—I had nothing to do with killing anybody.

> **Pete**

Vic, old pal, the Chief warned me, he said, "Pete, that Jones boy will try to turn the tables—put the blame on you." The Chief was sure right about that. Well, Vic, isn't gonna happen. The table won't be turnin'. Everyone in town knows the judge's son, that would be me, never would have killed some poor old guy. Mori, two more beers—I think my friend needs an extra-cold one.

(Mori walks over, picks up the other bottles and sets two fresh ones on the table)

So where does that leave us? If we both claim that the other person did it, we both go to jail. On the other hand, if one of us admits to causing the "accidental" death, then only that person would go to jail for say... 2 to 3 years.

Vic
Pete, are you really going to do this to me?

Pete
It's really about what you did to yourself. No one asked you to be my friend. You know I'm always gettin' into some kind of trouble—Ya lie down with dogs, ya gonna get fleas. By hangin' with me, you've been on the edge of trouble—it was bound ta happen.

Vic
My life is shit, Pete.

Pete
Don't get too dramatic. I told the Chief you were just fuckin' with the guy. He took a swing at you, you got pissed, picked up a piece of wood and clocked him in the head—down he goes, and in a panic, we ran away.

Vic
Sounds like you and the Chief have a plan.

Pete
The Chief did call my Mom and Dad and explained how "the accident" happened and "maybe" there could be an *arrangement* whereby you admitted that you had struck the old guy.

Vic
What kinda arrangement?

Pete

My Dad said that I could tell you that $10,000 would be
put in your college account **if...** you agreed that you were
the one who *accidentally* whacked the poor bastard.
Either way, Vic, you will have to do the time. If you don't
agree, I'll be doing some time with you. If you do agree,
you will still do a coupla years, but you will have $10,000
in your college account. I hate to rush you on this, but the
chief has to act now. He'll be here in a few minutes. Chief
will arrest you and me... or just you.
Whatta you say?

Vic *(thinking - takes a swig of beer)*

"Anybody can buy a car in whatever color they want... as
long it's black."

Pete

Not answering my question, Buddy.

Vic

It's a Hobson's Choice, Pete. I'll need $20,000, and I'll do
the deal.

Pete

Dad said I could go up to $15,000. If you don't take the
deal, he said that I could do the time with you—he also
said that it might do me some good (*Pete laughs*). There it
is Vic—$15,000 in your account or zip.

Vic *(has another hit of beer, lights a cigarette)*

The money has to be in my college account **before** I make
a full confession. And your Mom needs to send me a
lawyer. So there **you** have it—$15,000 in my account, and
a lawyer picked by your Mom. Then I'll make a
confession—I'll tell them that my *friend* Pete had nothing

to do with the guy getting *accidentally*... killed. Do we have a deal?

Pete
Let's drink to our deal, Vic—I'll even pick up the tab.

(Pete takes a drink of beer, then rocks back in his chair and raises both arms as a signal—Chief Harris enters the bar and walks toward Pete)

Police Chief Harris
Good evening Mr. Leknikov—thanks for bringing Mr. Jones along. Mr. Jones, I am Police Chief Harris and I assume that you know why I'm here.

Vic
Yes, sir, I do know. I want you to know that the whole incident was unintentional—it was a tragic... accident.

Police Chief Harris
I understand what happened last Friday night was, without a doubt, a terrible, terrible *accident*. Honesty is always the best approach, Mr. Jones. Now, if you don't mind, please stand. I will cuff you and take you to the station. After you meet with your lawyer we will talk in a little more detail.

(Vic stands up, the Chief puts the cuffs on, places his arm through Vic's elbow and escorts him out of the bar—as they are leaving...)

Pete *(loudly)*

Don't worry Vic, everything will be alright. The beer tab's on me.

Lights fade

End of Play

Acknowledgments

I have several people to thank for their help in preparing this third book of my trilogy.

First and foremost, my love and thanks to my wife Anne for her time and effort expended on the line drawings in the book as well as for her advice and editing suggestions.

My son Galen gets thanks for his work transforming the manuscript from Google Docs to Word, and for making the manuscript into a professional document.

I would also like to thank two friends who contributed poems to this book, namely, Carole Jenisch and Victoria Forsyth.

Lastly, I want to thank Tom Asacker for his advice and for his assistance with the cover design and layout.

About the Author

Robert Cruess was born in Mississippi, raised in Connecticut, worked in Venezuela, and has lived in New Hampshire with his wife and family for over forty years.

"Alone" is his third book of a collection of short stories and poems. His first book, "Time is all we have," was published in October 2017, and his second book, "On only nights," was published in December 2018.

He is a civil engineer, an award-winning developer, a writer, and, above all, a husband, father, and grandfather in love... with the life that he has.

Contact the author at rcruesspoet@gmail.com.